GOOD
GIFTS

Heidi Goehmann

Heidi Goehmann

writings on mental health, relationships, and Jesus

Introduction

Every year when winter drags on and on, I do my yearly pep talk to myself. This won't last forever, the snow, the cold, the dark. It's time for something new, I say. Most years, at about March 1st, I become so hungry for something *new*.

I'm ready for a new day, a new song, and to see a new landscape as I gaze out my kitchen window. While I know that *new* isn't always better, I think we were made for the knowledge of something to come, something waiting just around the corner. We live in eternity, you see, but we can't quite see it in the way we'd like, a blinding light in front of our faces. We can't hold eternity in our hands and walk around and show it to everyone. So, we live with eternity as an idea, a place saved for later. We call it heaven and we tuck it away for deathbeds and someday. We imagine golden gates and gemstones and a giant mansion made up of many, many rooms. In this mansion there's a giant deep freeze with pints and pints of coffee ice cream with dark chocolate and almond chunks, available for our enjoyment at any time. Ok, maybe that part is just my daydream.

While all of those things may be a sliver of the eternal, it isn't the full picture of what God has for us when He knit eternity in our hearts and sent Jesus to bring it to our souls. Eternity is now. Eternity is God with us. Eternity is Jesus sacrificing everything, then marking our foreheads and our hearts with Water and Word, and Him placing His Spirit inside of us. Eternity is that same Spirit flowing out like a mighty river to the world around us, grabbing onto someone else when I share the Word and all it has to say about His goodness and His gifts.

Jesus' brother, James, knew a little bit about Eternity. He regularly ate dinner with our Eternal Savior. He watched eternity walk around this earth right in front of him and heard the Word of the Promise straight from His mouth. And like all of Jesus' disciples, when His darkest hour came, He didn't stand beside what is eternal, because he was so worried about the pain of that day. I think we can all relate. This most likely is one reason why Jesus invites us to walk with the Son of God every day, walk in Eternal Life today, the next, and the next, rather than turning to it occasionally. This concept of concerning ourselves with eternity in our everyday life is written all over the book of James.

James is worried about a little thing called *congruence*. We all get locked up in incongruence at times. Incongruence is what happens when we deeply believe in eternity, but live without it in mind, like we are saving it for later.

Incongruence is what happens when we say we love God, but ignore our neighbor who is struggling with cancer, with addiction, or with any number of needs.

Incongruence is when we go to church but push aside making disciples for the ever-present to-do list of the day.

Incongruence is when I cannot for the life of me manage to bring the best parts of me to my family on a daily basis because of my lack of boundaries, self-control, and self-care.

I am incredibly incongruent. We all are. But the book of James teaches us that as we grow up into Christ, who is our Head, as we acknowledge and remember the eternity we have been offered today, not just tomorrow, we will become more and more congruent as we walk with Him.

Congruence is that blessed thing we see in our lives when we understand what we value and put it into action, rather than pushing it under the couch. Congruence is when we know Who our God is, and how He changes everything, including me.

Congruence happens when faith becomes life, rather than just part of our life.

Who's hungry for that? I know I am. In this life, we'll never be perfect, friends. Chief of sinners though we be, Jesus died so we can live in eternity now, rather than riddled with guilt and incongruence. This is the work we'll walk into with the book of James…we'll look at what we've been given and all the good in the gifts of God we never even knew He sat in front of us.

Join us for new.
Join us for congruent.
Join us for Good Gifts.

How to Use this Study

In all of my print studies, as with all the resources available on my website, I strive to create content that is easy to utilize, but also provides a consistent and thorough way to get into the Word in the middle of everyday life. My goal is for every study to be intensely theological, while being intensely practical, every time.

Each week, you can work through the Word in 3 ways:

Daily study readings:

Good Gifts is a six-week study. Each week, you will have the opportunity to work through various segments of the Book of James, alongside verses that interpret and connect for us throughout Scripture. There are four days of study to read each week. You can read it when and where you have the chance; if you miss a day of study in a week, not a big deal! Pick it up again, skip a day, or move to the next week. There is a whole lot of grace here. The goal is to *regularly* be in the Word, and that looks different for all of us. This study has questions embedded in the lessons. Try to answer them, but don't get too worked up if no answer comes for you. No one will be checking your answers. ;-)

Join or facilitate a small group:

Discussing the Word together gives us a firmer grasp on what God is speaking to us personally in that Word, as well as through one another's lives. Connection and community is a deep need God placed within each one of us. How we connect also looks different for each of us. Making a plan to discuss the Word over coffee with one friend, three friends, or making a formal study group with a set day and time, can bring the accountability we are looking for in our lives and a layer of enrichment and insight that can be surprising. You can also find video sessions to compliment this study on my YouTube channel – youtube.com/heidigoehmannwrites.

Scripture engagement and extras:
Drawing, taking notes, and journaling in the margins of this study book are welcomed and encouraged! Our brains are engaged more fully and for a longer period of time when we are given space for creative reflection. You will find a prayer walk and links to visual faith tools on the Good Gifts page at heidigoehmann.com, under the Studies Available tab.

I am so very thankful that you have chosen to invite me in and study the Word with me. I learn so much as I write each study, and even more when I hear from each of you! Do not hesitate to share your thoughts and insights with me by contacting me through the About page at heidigoehmann.com.

Happy studying!

The Good Giver

James 1:16-17
Do not be deceived, my beloved brothers.
Every good gift and every perfect gift is from above,
coming down from the Father of lights,
with whom there is no variation or shadow due to change.

week one

The Good Giver

Good Gifts from a Good Father
Welcome Adulthood, Send Some Wisdom Please
The Shock of Generosity
No One Sits in the Corner

Verse to consider

Every good gift and every perfect gift is from above, coming down from the Father of lights, with whom there is no variation or shadow due to change.

James 1:17

The Good Giver

day one

Good Gifts from a Good Father

God is good. It's just who He is, even when life comes in and makes it so hard to believe.

The Psalmist cries out in Psalm 136:1 –

> *Give thanks to the LORD, for He is good, for His steadfast love endures forever.*

In the book of Exodus, Moses asked for God's glory and God showed Moses all His goodness instead. This was a grace move on God's part. Moses actually got goodness instead of full-on glory because God's glory is so much it would kill us mere mortals. But God did give Moses goodness overload. You can read the full account in Exodus 33:13-23. How do glory and goodness meet in this account?

In Mark 10:17-18, Jesus clarifies for us, in great humility, without revealing his position as God-in-human-flesh, that goodness can only come in and through God the Father:

And as he was setting out on his journey, a man ran up and knelt before him and asked him, "Good Teacher, what must I do to inherit eternal life?" And Jesus said to him, "Why do you call me good? No one is good except God alone.

Aka – "You won't find goodness elsewhere, Kind Sir. What exactly is it you are really looking for?"

What are we really looking for when we look for good?

Do we want *stuff* that's good?

Do we want to *feel* good?

Do we want a good reputation, a good job, a good future?

All these things are nice, but they aren't necessarily good, because good only comes from a Good Father. We know this, because we have the book of James to hold in our hands, to digest, and to study over the next six weeks.

For this week, bookmark James chapter one and get cozy with it. Read the whole chapter one time through. It's a gem and we'll rest in it our whole first week of study. Today, we'll focus in on James 1:16-17 in particular –

> *Do not be deceived, my beloved brothers. Every good gift and every perfect gift is from above, coming down from the Father of lights, with whom there is no variation or shadow due to change.*

James connects some dots for us. God's not just Good, he's a Father to us, and He's not just a Father to us, He's a Good one. God's goodness is wrapped in Fatherly affection and His Fatherly affection is all kinds of goodness.

God is who He says He is, but the devil wants to deceive us; sometimes believing God and His goodness is another thing entirely.

The goodness of God can be particularly hard to believe for anyone with an extremely imperfect, or even terrible, earthly father. God is perfect in every way in His role as Father. Still, there are many things in life that feel less than good. It's easy to piece those things together and create in our head a God who isn't for our good. Disease, shootings, poverty, bankruptcy, family turmoil…they all demand accounting for. Who's responsible around here anyway?

We can rest in the Truth of Scripture that tells us over and over again, in the midst of life chaos, in the seasons we feel pummeled by storms: God is still good. He is the Father of Lights, not darkness. He is the Father of Lights, not darkness. James reminds us, "Do not be deceived, beloved brothers." We trust in God's good Word.

God is not only good. He is steadfast, according to James.

The devil is a shifty one, but God neither shifts nor changes. What does Hebrews 13:8 have to say about God's nature?

2:10   Never Changes

The devil aims to deceive us into believing that God is unsure and unsafe. This deception pulls and stretches us. It leaves us feeling doubtful, questioning whether God will meet our needs. James 1:17 reminds us of the steadfastness of God by referencing the all too familiar evening shadows. The Greek root word for variation in James 1:17 is related to change, variation, or even mutation. Let the Word assure you – God does not mutate. The devil may make himself into a snake to fool us, but God does not try to trick us. James tells us that is not in our Father's nature to fool. God has His own will and He is subject to no one. He lays His will out for us in His Word: He created us. He saves us through Jesus. He sustains us. He's coming back for us. He's with us through the Spirit in the meantime. Redemption, life, forgiveness, and salvation are found in Jesus and Jesus alone, and this is always at the heart of God's will.

At the end of our study day today, I'll leave you with this: Consider all the good things of God that you can think of. Try to list at least ten of the good things about God, or ten good things that God brings into your life. Then close with the simple prayer below.

always there
takes care of me
loves me when it isn't easy
doesn't change
gave me great family
God is love + grace

Father, You are good. Jesus, Your good sacrifice saves us. Spirit, may Your goodness fill us today. In Jesus' name we pray, Amen.

The Good Giver

day two
Welcome Adulthood,
Send Some Wisdom Please

Wisdom isn't something we usually seek early on in life. We generally like smart. We'll take brains, maybe some beauty, a little charisma, if you please, but the desire for wisdom seems to delay itself. Somewhere at about, "Oh goodness, I need to choose a life path, a college, a career, a place to live..." That's when we start to look around for lady wisdom to walk alongside us on the path. And oh but do we need wisdom! There are so many choices in life! It's easy to get weighed down by concern over our ability to ever make a "right" decision. We either let anxiety take its hold or we try to throw off our concerns with a *laissez faire* approach, "Who cares! You only live once!" which works for the moment, but comes with some pretty stiff consequences over time.

If we're being honest, neither of these approaches really work. God speaks plainly through James to gives us another, better answer. Wisdom rests solely in the hands of our Creator, and He offers us a direct connection to where we will find that wisdom. Please read James 1:5-8. Where does this passage encourage us to go when we lack wisdom?

To God

Things in this world decompose. Flowers wither. Companies collapse. Buildings deteriorate. Everything around us is unstable.

Yesterday in our study, we learned about what, or rather Who, is stable: the Lord. He is steadfast and never-changing. Wisdom is related to God's stability, in a way that *smart* or *intelligent* isn't. God invites us to partake in His wisdom in James 1:5-8, and He steadfastly gives it to us when we ask. He gives us His Spirit to work in our inner being. He leaves the Word open and available to us at all times. And this wisdom works not just in big life-changing events, but in times of transition, in wrestling and decision-making times, and in the every day. It impacts how we interact with others, how we lead, how we parent, and where we spend our money.

Where do you see God's wisdom working in your days?

Luke 21 helps us understand further the wisdom God offers us. Read Luke 21:10-18 in your Bible. What is different about God's wisdom from the world's according to this passage?

not to follow man but God

Well, that seems risky, doesn't it? How in the world do we move forward in life without settling things beforehand in our minds? This passage seems like the opposite of wisdom. Let's reframe these verses with the whole Word of God in mind. When we have an active relationship with God the Father, Son, and Holy Spirit, our connection to the Word alive and well in us makes all the difference. Double-mindedness and instability go by the wayside, when we fix our eyes on Jesus. We make mistakes, but there's forgiveness and forgiveness itself has the shape of wisdom.

The disciples were entering into a time of persecution in Luke 21. I'm sure they wanted assurance and security more than ever, just as we do in our own lives. Jesus' answer to them is –

Lean on me. Come to me. Meditate on me.

The decisions we need to make will get made as they need to get made. The real substance of abundant life is in knowing the One Who is truly Wise.

The world will not stop being crazy until Jesus comes again. Decisions won't stop coming rapid-fire most days. Adulting will likely never feel like kittens, roses, and unicorns. The only thing we can control is where we go when we need help. When all those decisions are coming toward us, where do we turn?

As I get older, and maybe a little wiser, my prayers have changed from a lot of words, to prayers with my Bible open and something much more simple:

"Here You go, Lord. I have no idea, Lord. But I know You do, Lord."

Hand it to Him and trust in the same Spirit Christ Jesus sent to literally light His disciples on fire. He is ready to give you wisdom at every turn and every bend in the road. Every good and perfect gift is from above…including wisdom.

day three
The Shock of Generosity

The youth group at our church in Ohio was known to have some zany ideas. One year, we were robbed of our Christmas caroling plans by a massive snow storm. We were bummed, but we found solace in hot cocoa, popcorn, and Christmas movies. Fast forward to Easter and we were still bummed. Enter one of my finest ideas ever - Easter caroling! And not just any Easter caroling, but Easter caroling to deliver baskets of encouragement to workers at local fast food restaurants.

We were so jazzed. We practiced our Easter ditty, "Up, Up, Up, He Arose," gathered our Easter goodies to share, and invited along friends and friends of friends. We organized restaurant stops and planned out our progressive dinner style stops based on the fast food menus. First stop: side salads. We walked up to the cashier to order and asked if we could sing her a carol (no need to freak anyone out in our excitement to share). We sang her our Easter tune and offered up an Easter basket of Gospel and chocolate goodies, sharing our thanks for her willingness to work in our community and for taking our order with kindness.

The look on that woman's face I will never forget. There were actual tears in her eyes. It was like Bob Barker or Drew Carey had called her down for the showcase showdown.

"For me?" she asked.

"Yes, for you."

"Why?"

"Because, God loves you and we just wanted you to know."

"But, there's lots of stuff in here. Should I share it?"

"That's up to you. But this basket is for you. We wanted you to know that Jesus died and rose for you. Happy Easter!"

We are not freakishly generous people. We aren't special messengers from God. We entered a restaurant and gave a gift. We did the same at three more restaurants and got many of the same responses.

People are surprised by even remotely generous behavior. I think the idea of generosity almost makes us nervous in our current cultural context. What will people want from me in return? What will they expect from me? Generosity brings up all our "I'm not worthy" instincts. But generosity is a huge part of the message of the Gospel of Jesus Christ. We have a generous Father. He loved us first and He loves us more. In fact, He loves us most.

What this generosity does in our lives, and the lives of others, may surprise us. Look up James 1:17 again and underline each instance of the word *every* you find in the verse.

James does not say *some*. He does not say *a few*. He doesn't say *many* gifts. James says *every* and the word *every* means something: God is shockingly generous of Himself. You'll hear James talk again and again, throughout the book, about how we respond to this in the Spirit.

The generosity of an "every" kind of God wells up in us and pours out to the world. This world could do with some "every", because they're so used to "scarcely".

James 1:19-27 gives us an interesting view of generosity by addressing God's generous spirit in ways we don't often see. Read the passage and answer this question – What does God show us in the mirror?

That we arent good we need to follow him

When God generously shows us who we are in the mirror, we may not always love what we see. He shows us both our sinfulness and our need for salvation, but He also shows us our beauty as His creation and the mark of the cross eternally etched on our forehead.

God's generosity isn't limited to love. He also gives honesty, sincerity, steadfastness, hope, joy, courage, and more.

He generously gives us purpose, rather than a void. We hear the Word and then He generously gives us work to complete, vocations to fulfill, grace to be shared.

When you look in the mirror and see your strengths and your weaknesses, what kind of generosity is God pouring in you today?

How might the thing you are generously receiving from Him reach others around you and impact them?

Maybe it's generosity of affection, generosity or discernment, generosity of care or kindness, or generosity of time. Let Him work in you. The implanted Word has saved you. Now let it reach out to every single person you meet, whether it's your family and friends, or a cashier at the store. Who is someone you feel called to share a touch of generosity with today?

That just might be the person who needs to see His generosity the most today.

The Good Giver

day four
No One Sits in the Corner

How many of us are familiar with the discipline method of putting children in a corner? Do you have any memories of receiving or experiencing this discipline method yourself?

At its best, I think this method is intended to give children a time out to contemplate their words or their choices and then be welcomed back into the social activity of a household with forgiveness and grace. We all could use a good time out at times for sure! But at its worst, the corner represents for some children (and adults by proxy) a place of shame and of loneliness. Without loving relationships wrapped around us and discipline evoked with great care and privacy, children have spirits which are easily crushed. Discipline is certainly important, and the corner may even have its place, but truth is always balanced with love and justice with compassion, particularly in family life.

Sometimes life feels like we've been put in a corner. We feel less-than at work, at home, in our families, in our communities, or at

church. On our worst days our internal monologue sounds something like this –
Do I matter?

Do I have anything worthwhile to contribute?

Am I included or forgotten?

Part of the discipline of the corner is the creation of the desire within a child to be reconnected. We want someone to reach out their hand and bring us out from the corner. We want someone to say, "You are welcome here."

The problem comes when we compare and contrast our invitations to everyone around us. We end up asking for others *to matter less* because we think somehow this raises our own worth in the eyes of God, our parents, or others who matter most to us. We end up quietly, or not so quietly, resentful.

James hands us the mirror and says, "Partiality is not working for you."

Read James 2:1-7 and see this struggle played out in the Christian church during the first century. They were sinners too, redeemed by the same God. What was the impact of partiality in the early Christian church?

James is going to have none of this sitting-in-the-corner business. First, he reminds those early believers who they are as followers of Christ. James tells them to hold this faith, hold their position in the Kingdom of God. Christ in us changes things. Christ always shakes things up wherever He goes, including our hearts and minds. We do not exist as the world exists because of

Christ in us. We remain steadfast by holding onto Him, by holding to our faith in Him, rather than whatever praise or honor or lifting up the world would offer.

Hebrews 12:1-3 is helpful for understanding more on the change of perspective we have because the Spirit is helping us hold to faith in Jesus. I like the NIV translation for this passage:

> *Therefore, since we are surrounded by such a great cloud of witnesses, let us throw off everything that hinders and the sin that so easily entangles. And let us run with perseverance the race marked out for us, fixing our eyes on Jesus, the pioneer and perfecter of faith. For the joy set before him he endured the cross, scorning its shame, and sat down at the right hand of the throne of God. Consider him who endured such opposition from sinners, so that you will not grow weary and lose heart.*

It's easy to lose heart, to feel like we're sitting in a corner and no one notices. Jesus does. Jesus offers us the very best seat in His heart, as cheesy as it sounds, and so the other stuff, the need to be better than or higher than someone else, in order to be noticed, can be thrown off or as the ESV puts it, *lain aside.* Our selfish need, wanting less for other people, now sits in the corner.

If Jesus is invited, all that other junk isn't, and that's perfect because it wasn't needed anyway. Jesus fills in everything. He is the author and perfecter...Son of our good Father who has all the good gifts.

James 1:9-11 reminds us we are all just grass on this earth. We will perish in the blink of an eye. Whether we're beautiful, smart, well-behaved, the most fun person at the party, what have you, we're all the same in Christ Jesus.

Christ puts no one in a corner. He raises people up in His death and resurrection.

Who can we also raise up? We can make a difference in this world by holding the faith, rather than holding on to our own need for "special"? Christ is seated in the best place, so we can invite others to come near to His throne rather than sitting in the corner.

No one sits in the corner in the church, literally or metaphorically. Discipline will come, but compassion will reign. Relationships will be wrapped in grace, even as truth comes through every conversation that includes His Word. Christ rolls out the banquet feast and aren't we blest to hand out the invitations?

James 1:16-17
Do not be deceived, my beloved brothers.
Every good gift and every perfect gift is from above,
coming down from the Father of lights,
with whom there is no variation or shadow due to change.

week two

Good Mercy

Liberty, Freedom, and the Pursuit of Jesus
The Forgotten Gift of Warmth
The Good Gift of Peace
The Wisdom Default

Verse for consideration

For judgment is without mercy to one who has shown no mercy. Mercy triumphs over judgment.

James 2:13

day one

Liberty, Freedom, and the Pursuit of Jesus

Galatians 5:1 holds a powerful reminder for our lives. I heard it
first in the NIV translation, at a time when I desperately needed
some freedom, so that translation always is a bit stickier for me
when I'm laden down with expectations and the burdens of the
day or season -

> *It is for freedom that Christ has set us free. Stand*
> *firm, then, and do not let yourselves be burdened again by*
> *a yoke of slavery.*

The apostle Paul feels so strongly about this concept that his
next words are highlighted with an exclamation point or other
special indicators in many translations:

> *Mark my words!* (NIV)
> *Listen!* (NLT)
> *Look:* (ESV)
> *Take note!* (HCSB)

Paul isn't the only one concerned about Christian freedom.
James also tackles the topic of Christian freedom and we have

so much to learn from him. Freedom, like much of the Christian walk, is intricately tied to the good gift of mercy we receive from our good Father, through His good Son, our Savior.

Read James 2:8-13. What do you notice first about the subject of freedom in this passage? (There are no wrong answers here.)

I happened to notice how many times James uses the word *law*. Look through the text again, and note the places James reminds us that the law exists. Sometimes it's good to be reminded that the law isn't really something we can ignore. We could try, but it wouldn't get us anywhere but to disappointment valley. The law is weighty, to be taken seriously – but without it, freedom does not exist.

The world's definition of freedom is in the *absence* of responsibility, the absence of work, the absence of caring, and the absence of giving. With this model, our attempts to throw off life, to break free from any and all expectations surrounding us, tightens up the very shackles we were hoping to escape.

God's law is not the problem. Do not hurt other people, do not betray your spouse by committing adultery, love God with your whole heart – these are not oppressive, and they are not outdated. These are not asking too much. The world is safer with God's law in it. Our hearts are safer with the law in them. The problem is that we try to find answers to our failures of the law within ourselves or other people. We also try to pursue the law, pointing at the few points we can keep, in order to make us feel better about the gaping holes we tear in other parts of it.

We try to get the law to change our situations. We think the law applied to others will solve our problems and will solve this world's problems. For instance, when someone treats us poorly, we gossip to someone else about it and we freeze out friendship, storing up our hurt. When we're confronted with poverty, we become aggressive, concerned for our own resources, rather than the needs of others that God has put before us. We argue with our spouse and cast blame. That's all the law at work. Sin sits like an elephant in every room we inhabit and every room our neighbor inhabits. So, what's the alternative to throwing the law around to try to make things better?

Write James 2:10 out below to zero in on the Truth.

We are continually pursuing justice, but the pursuit of Jesus is so much better.

Perfection, whether in ourselves or in others, isn't what the King of Kings asks in us. Perfection is what the law asks for us to be. The law is necessary, but Jesus met what the law required with mercy.

Mercy's name is Jesus.

God *expects* us to follow the law.

But God also…
>…expected to send Christ into the world.
>…expected to give Him the load of expectation we could never carry.
>…expected to roll the stone away.
>…expected to triumph.
>…expected for mercy to win.

God's expect-ations are our gain in Jesus Christ.

James gives us a clearer picture of the law, a whole picture of the law, when it's coupled with what God intended for it to be coupled with - the sweet Gospel grace of our Savior.

Our expectations put our weighed down hearts in the grave. God's expectations and God's law all point us to Christ Jesus, so we can embrace real and genuine freedom. The law of liberty is being honest with ourselves and others, knowing we can't keep one bit of the law, and looking to Jesus every day, every hour, every second to fill in all our gaps and let His mercy reign. It makes us call out judgement when we see it and feel it and say,

No way!

Not invited.

You may be excused now.

How is God's mercy different from what the world offers us or expects from us?

The law of liberty also keeps us kind, knowing that our neighbor sure and certainly cannot keep the law either. Christ reigns for them too. It makes us want to pass out mercy rather than hoarding it up for ourselves. After all, what's freedom if it's not free?

Friends, family members, store clerks, church members, coworkers – they will fail us. But that means we get to show them that mercy wins. Mercy is so much bigger and better than junky old expectations.

James spurs us on. He helps us to see how the law and the gospel fit together so we can speak and act as one who knows and believes in both. That's congruence.

I pray that today you can embrace a little more freedom - for yourself and for your neighbor. Let that mercy reign. And when it's hard, pursue Him, run toward His throne.

John 8:36 reminds us of our liberty as well –

So if the Son sets you free, you will be free indeed.

Free indeed. Less judgement, more mercy. Mercy triumphs.

Good Mercy

day two

The Forgotten Gift of Warmth

This January we bought a house that was built in 1885. I love it. It has nine-foot ceilings, hobbit doorways, and comes in just under 1000 square feet. It's very "us" and I wouldn't trade it in for the world.

I do miss warmth though.

Any historic homeowner knows the struggle of trying to stay warm. Yesterday I dared to crank up my heat to a wild and aggressive 72 degrees, lest I actually freeze to death in my own home. Hot tea is no longer a nice little luxury, but a necessity for warming your hands on cold, cloudy days. I layer on my cabin socks, my chunky Irish knit sweater, my slippers, and, let's be real, sometimes a hat. I grumble and then I look out my front window and am reminded just what a lucky girl I am. I am blessed with a home, blankets, socks and a family to fill my life with all kinds of joy. I am blessed to have hats and scarves when necessary and blessed to crank up the heat to 75 if I so desired and still be able to pay the bill, albeit reluctantly. All these are good gifts from God, but God wouldn't be any less God if I didn't have a single one of them. It's easier to say, and harder to live, when you're in a place of physical need.

James 2:14-17 talks a lot about need, particularly the needs we have and see around us for clothes and food and the stuff of daily life. What all of those things add up to, however, when you think about it is one gift – the good gift of warmth.

Read James 2:14-17 and describe this gift of warmth James is talking about in the passage.

I have a theory about this passage: when we look at this passage our eyes and ears immediately go to the word dead. It's natural. It's a shocking and dramatic word for us. Couple it with a big word like faith and all kinds of anxiety starts poking out. We also don't want the relationship between faith and works to be misunderstood. It's important that we don't pile up expectations on ourselves (see yesterday's study) or act as though God couldn't care less about our life here on earth, so we spend so much time explaining verse 17 that we never get around to hashing out verses 14-16. We glide over the simple words – clothes and food – and settle on the bigger words – peace, faith, works – haphazardly giving them a place of higher importance simply because they require some theological explanation.

Today, I want to talk about warmth. Warmth is a little word, mundane and basic. James imitates the flippancy of a person who is slapping a bandage on a person's gushing wound in verse 16.

The gushing wound in our current cultural context is warmth.

We may (or may not) be clothing the homeless, feeding the impoverished and caring for a brother or sister in need, but I think our bigger problem is warmth. Christ Jesus is not only loving, caring, compassionate, holy, good, and true. He is warm. He takes time for people. He invites people in, even when he knows it's going to hurt, when there will be loss, when there will be betrayal, when there will be drama.

Our time and energy are limited. It's important to start somewhere though. How can we show Gospel-bred warmth to our spouse, to our families, to the people we live with, to our neighbors, and to those we share space with on this globe.

What if "Go in peace" turned to "Come, let me help you see His peace."?

The Greek word for *be warmed* back in James 2:16 is *thermainesthe*. It's related to our word for thermos. What if it was as simple as sharing food with someone rather than handing them food, or shopping for a coat with someone rather than putting it in a collection bin. What if we invited a friend over, into our stack of dirty dishes and cluttered chaos, rather than, well...not inviting anyone over.

The world is hungry for warmth and warmth is a door to the Gospel. It was true at the time of Jesus, true at the time of James, and it remains true today.

Read Matthew 14:13-21 in your Bible. What kinds of things does Jesus do that offer warmth to the people?

Jesus sees our own need for Help. He gives us the Holy Spirit. This Spirit-filled warmth lives in our hearts and souls so we can share it. If you're like me, you have a to-go coffee tumbler or thermos tucked away somewhere. Let's put them to use today. Bring a warm beverage to someone in your life. It's simple, I know. But it's a start. Life-giving Gospel sharing is built on life lived together and that starts with some warmth. Go meet a neighbor. Bring a fresh bag of something tasty. Put a Bible verse of encouragement with it. Bring a pot of tea to boil and pack it in a thermos for that mid-afternoon slump at work, then share it around and share a little bit of yourself and Jesus in the process.

When has someone shared the gift of warmth with you?

How can we connect the warmth that we share with the message of Christ, be it immediate or over time in relationship?

We are free, friends. Free to live different, to take time, and to open our chilly but wonderful homes and lives to those around us.

day three
The Good Gift of Peace

We are given a great amount of freedom in this life. Yesterday, we covered the freedom to be warm, to invite others in, to be in meaningful relationship rather than in the loneliness vacuum. We also have the freedom to believe what we would believe, even in the face of very real oppression in various corners of the world. We have the freedom to dance in the face of trial, to laugh when evil rears its ugly head, because we know a God who is bigger, who is smarter, and frankly who is better than any of it.

Knowing Him doesn't give us these freedoms – they were there all along. But knowing God introduces us to these freedoms, opens our eyes to the freedoms we would miss otherwise. Read 2 Corinthians 3:16-17 to see how this works. Who opens our eyes to freedom according to those verses?

The veil is removed. If you look further back in the same chapter of Scripture, the apostle Paul tells us we get to be bold about that freedom by the same Spirit. Write 2 Corinthians 3:12 below to give it some space in our minds.

I love bold. Bold speaks my language. Soapboxes don't bother me, nor do heated discussions.

James reminds us again that there are two sides to every coin. As Christians, we don't just see one side in life, in conversation, or in any given situation. The veil is removed. We can speak boldness and we can speak peace. We are free to see both sides together.

What does James 3:2-12 teach us about these two sides of our words?

We all have some words. Some of us have more than others. Sometimes our words are helpful, sometimes they would be better off tucked away with our tongue against the side of our cheek, mouth closed.

Let's connect some dots. Read James 3:18. Consider the balance of peace alongside boldness. How is peace connected to any of the following, mentioned by James? Write your thoughts alongside each of them.

a tongue setting the world ablaze

a ship of words that stays the course rather than being blown by the winds of life-change and internal roiling emotion

words of sustenance for someone's soul, rather than words of poison

words tamed in the knowledge of the righteousness bestowed by Jesus

salt water or fresh water

fresh fruit or rotten fruit

James's point isn't that we will never be angry, or that we will never need to go forth and proclaim truth boldly. By all means, boldly go. But there are two sides to the coin. Even bold faith looks peaceable in Christ Jesus. The battle has been won. The victory claimed. We're not fighting for it anymore. We just share it. We just confess it. Confessing is what helps us balance boldness and peace. We have a rudder, like James says. His name is Jesus. His Spirit guides our hearts and our lives and our words. Confessing is simply letting Christ guide, keeping Him at the center. Because the victory is won, we have the time to consider our words in prayer before letting them roll off our tongue. Where do you need boldness today? Where do you need peace?

Dear Lord, help me find the boldness and help me find the peace, all in You.

day four
The Wisdom Default

When reformer, theologian, and pastor Martin Luther referenced the book of James early in his ministry, he was what we would call, "not a fan." It has been said that Luther went so far as to call it a "gospel of straw," judging it difficult to swallow and lacking in gospel grace.

One of Luther's complaints about the book, supporting the famous "straw" comment, was that he found the book of James to be disorganized. Sometimes when I sit drinking my coffee and reading the book of James myself, I can give some credence to Luther's fire on the topic. James does appear jumpy at first glance. Without sparing too much time for Heidi's wonderings, I lean toward the possibility that James is worked up. Whenever people feel passionately about what they are saying, their words can have some jump to them, certainly. The words of the Bible are Holy Spirit inspired words, yet still contain the individuality of their writers. Historians tell us Luther felt much differently about the book of James as he aged. My study Bible explains that the book grew on Martin Luther, so to say. As he studied it and maybe even as he experienced more life, Luther began to see the law and gospel truth in James's words.

After studying the book of James longer, I have also discovered that it is not as disorganized as it first appears. All the chapters in James reflect back on chapter one, which is primarily about God's character –

God is steadfast.

God is generous.

God is impartial.

God is wise.

James then talks about these subjects with repetition within the book – steadfastness of faith; generosity; impartiality; wisdom, particularly in the area of testing and trials; Christian freedom; and taming the tongue.

We studied each of these aspects of God's character in week one of our study. Any time you are reading through James and you hear too much law, too much fire, or the words seem too hard to choke down, flip back to James chapter one. Rest in God's perfection and be reminded that He gives us the Spirit. Jesus calls the Spirit "Helper" for a reason. We need some help! And we have that help in a God who saves, a God who is steadfast, generous, and wise, a God who is impartial.

Today's topic does not disappoint as far as James's style goes. It contains some fire, but the conclusion of James's words reminds us that through the fire of the truth, we get to the sweet, sweet Gospel of forgiveness, grace, and good fruit.

Let's dive in. Please read James 3:13-18. Note any words with negative connotation as you read, words that seem like harsh truth or difficult things to deal with in people.

James is the friend you call when you need someone to tell it like it is.

Sometimes what we call wisdom is actually far from it. Sometimes our wisdom is filled with our own ideas and ambitions. This is wisdom that is not directed by the Word of God. We have been culprits, as well as recipients, of this kind of wisdom. When a friend asks advice, how do we dispense it? Do we pray with them? Do we open the Bible and try to find answers alongside of them?

It sounds so separated from what we usually do in this world that we may get a little embarrassed picturing it – praying, bringing the Word into the conversation. It sounds cheesy to say to a friend,

"Have you looked in the Bible?"

"I'm wondering what God has to say about this problem?"

"One time, when I was struggling, Philippians 4 really helped me."

We may point to Christ, but for the most part it isn't our default. James gives us a new idea-

Let's make the Word of God, the wisdom of God, our default.

James uses some strong words, some harsh words in James 3 - vile, disordered, demonic - yikes.

Hear him out. Wisdom changes lives, but when we offer only what we know, what we think, or what we want to see happen, that's the devil working overtime. It's sinful and it's selfish and it's distracting.

What are some gentle ways you have shared the Word with people who are seeking wisdom?

Double back to James 3:17. What seven characteristics can be found in good wisdom, God's wisdom?

It's pure – It's God's ideas I'm sharing, His wisdom – not polluted by my wants for my friend and this world's suggestions.

It's peaceable – It seeks peace, it's not seeking to hurt anyone, it isn't ramped up to go for the jugular with vengeance.

It's gentle – It talks nicely, with kindness, keeping the person's individual needs in mind.

It's open to reason – It can have a conversation. It understands that answers take time and searching, wrestling. It's not offended by debate, especially when someone is angry or hurting.

It's full of mercy and good fruit – It gives space for frustration and mourning, it's ready to give grace when it's needed, even if it hasn't been asked for. When it's put to work, there will be visible or invisible goodness as the outcome.

It's impartial and sincere – It's not for my good, or your good, or another friend's good. It's for His good, for everyone's good as children valued by God.

Go back and circle or put a star by the one characteristic that sticks with you most today. Wisdom isn't easy. I almost cringe when someone asks for my thoughts or advice because I do it so poorly. I like my ideas, but I'm learning to let Him lead. I'm learning to open the Word in my own life and in life together with others, to share and grow and let His wisdom flow.

He knows so much better anyway. Wouldn't you agree?

James 1:16-17
Do not be deceived, my beloved brothers.
Every good gift and every perfect gift is from above,
coming down from the Father of lights,
with whom there is no variation or shadow due to change.

week three

Good Fruit

Grocery Shopping and the Fruit of Forgiveness
No Chameleons Welcome
The Good Fruit of Correction
Different Fruits for Different Folks

Verse for consideration

But the wisdom from above is first pure,
then peaceable, gentle, open to reason, full of
mercy and good fruits, impartial and sincere.

James 3:17

day one
Grocery Shopping and the Fruit of Forgiveness

I love the produce department at the grocery store. It's full of colors and textures. There are piles of almost-ripe bananas and see-through containers of any kind of berry you could want. Displays are round and square and triangular. It smells fresh. Sometimes if you inhale just right there's a snap of citrus for the sinuses.

The biggest bummer about the produce department is that there are seasons. I live in America. I can get what crazy outlandish fruit I want, when I want it, but it may be four times the price or have traveled across miles and miles to over-ripeness, because fruit can't be controlled by my desires and whims. I could buy blackberries right now, but only if I want to break the bank. And if I want a ruby red grapefruit in the middle of the summer, I'm gonna pay.

God's fruit is unlike the fruit at the supermarket. It doesn't have a season or region. It just is. But *like* the fruit at the store, I can't demand what I want and get exactly that. Fruit grows when and where it will, based on God's plans. Still, God promises, as baptized children of God, we will never be without His fruit because it is of His Spirit. This week, we'll discover all kinds of tidbits about God's fruit in us and for us. James highlights a few different fruits in particular that come from a God who plants Himself in us. We have a God who waters and grows and builds up throughout our days.

Turn to James 2:17-20, to remember a discourse central to James's viewpoint of fruit.

> So also faith by itself, if it does not have works, is dead. But someone will say, "You have faith and I have works." Show me your faith apart from your works, and I will show you my faith by my works. You believe that God is one; you do well. Even the demons believe—and shudder! Do you want to be shown, you foolish person, that faith apart from works is useless?

The word written as *work* in our translation is from the Greek root word ergon - an action that carries with it the desire within. It's not just work, it's work done with purpose. It's work done with the knowledge of the Creator. This is one reason we call it fruit. It's the natural growth of the tree planted and watered by Christ in our baptisms. As we read the Word and worship together, we grow and grow and grow some more.

Have you ever had a day that felt like there was no fruit? Look back at James 1:17. Just how certain and sure is our Creator and Lord, according to James?

Our work is steadfast because He is steadfast. Our work is a sure thing, because He is as certain as the sun – actually more so. The physical manifestation of His steadfastness, i.e. the Spirit put inside of us, transforms us into doers. We can certainly dig our feet in – God gives us free will; but when we're living life in the Word, God is constantly transforming. We don't have to wonder whether the fruit will come. According to Matthew 7:24-25, what does the fruit of a steadfast doer look like?

When was a time you remained steadfast when the metaphoric rains fell?

With the Holy Spirit living inside of us, we aren't shifting shadows. Let's honor the times we have *remained* for a moment. Sometimes these times include big struggle, but mostly, the remaining is part of the ordinary life of faith in Jesus. Yes, we are sinners. There have surely been times we have separated ourselves from the Word, whether by avoiding opening it or listening with one ear closed. It becomes harder (not impossible, mind you) but harder to be doers of the Word, producing bountiful fruit, with our Bible shut and ears stopped up. How do fruit trees fare in a drought? Not so well, I hear. What have you experienced or seen happen in a time of drought from the Word, whether self-imposed or because of unforeseen circumstances?

Jesus puts all the pieces together for us and brings us the salvation we need, come what may. In our constant state of existing as sinful people in a sinful world, God offers a remarkable, yet often overlooked, fruit. What is the often-overlooked fruit mentioned in Luke 3:8?

Whether we can see the fruit of God in us or not, whether we feel like the produce department at the grocery store or the dried and cracking field of a too hot, too dry summer, we simply turn to Him in repentance every day if we want to see fruit. The gift of repentance, and the fruit it produces, is so often overlooked.

Repentance is a big word, and big words are intimidating, let alone the idea of looking deeper into our sins and the brokenness of the world. Sometimes, when we feel overwhelmed and we can spot Satan trying to bring the shame in, it's ok to keep it simple. My simplest acts of repentance sound like this:

Lord, I have failed to love you and your Word most. Lord, I have hurt others and put myself first so many times. Lord, open my heart to hear you, follow you, and know you more each day in Jesus Christ.

Now, write your own prayer of repentance. Whether simple or detailed, be assured that God hears and brings fruit.

Christ is faithful. The Spirit in us is steadfast, not a shifting shadow. Forgiveness is a wild and wonderfully prolific fruit that brings Life and Salvation and it is a fruit which brings other fruits! In taking the time to admit our sin, we can be more aware of the work He is doing in our lives on any given day. Look – He offered forgiveness when I yelled at my kids. Look – He offered forgiveness when I avoided my neighbor. Look – He offered forgiveness when...you could fill in a thousand blanks.

Repentance keeps us steadfast in the Spirit, turning back, turning back, and turning back again to a God who loves us.

The grocery store produce section holds nothing on God's bounty.

day two
No Chameleons Welcome

When I was young, I dated a guy that I would classify as a chameleon. You never knew what you were going to get. I have spent many a night lamenting the choices of my youth, but in Christ, we all learn and grow from even our rotten choices. As I have aged, one thing that God has shown me in my own need to repent and be forgiven every day, was this:

It takes a chameleon to know a chameleon.

By that I mean, part of the reason I was attracted to guys who changed colors and shapes like they changed outfits, was that when I looked deep down, I did as well. This is to some extent developmentally appropriate for middle schoolers and high schoolers, but there's a time to grow up. Developmentally, pre-teens and teens try on personalities, ideas, and opinions daily. Part of growing is growing out of our chameleon skin. The chameleon in us is part of what Paul calls spiritual infancy. What does Paul have to say about spiritual infancy in 1 Corinthians 3:1-3?

Paul's admonishments are also encouragements. We are ready. We are growing. We are big and brave enough with Christ in us to let God flush out the chameleon pieces still stuck inside of us. In today's lesson, James will teach us about being one whole person, rather than a chameleon with shifting and changing fruit. James addresses this chameleon issue in almost every chapter.

Look through the following passages in James to get an overview. Although each passage addresses different topics, you'll see the chameleon effect running through all of them. After each segment, write how you see the chameleon effect around you in the world.

James 1:5-8
James discusses how easy it is for us to be doubtful in prayer and what we ask from God. We believe He is capable, but live wondering if He's capable.

James 3:9-10
James addresses the tendency for our tongue to run one way and then another on any given day.

James 4:8-10
James addresses our failure to admit our sinfulness, while identifying the irony that facing our guilt and shame allows God to exalt us in forgiveness. We haphazardly try to present a version of ourselves to others that doesn't "need" forgiveness.

James 5:12
*James calls out the chameleon in each of us point blank.
We like to say no when we mean yes, and yes when we
mean no.*

Growing up means looking at the world honestly, but it also means looking at ourselves honestly. Where in our life do we present ourselves differently to please others? Where do we put Him in a box and forget about Him? Where are we shining God's light?

The good news is that fruit comes from our Savior and His Spirit, and is not determined by our efforts alone, whether consistent or inconsistent. We are given the gift of His fruit even when we fail. We confess and are forgiven, our hands are cleaned, and then we grow. We shed that chameleon coat and when it pops back on, we turn to God and ask Him to continue the hard work of molting it off us.

Good Fruit

day three
The Good Fruit of Correction

Not many of us like correction. Our distaste for correction starts as small children. What were you like as a child? Were you easily corrected or a little more rebellious by nature?

As adults, we might understand correction a bit more, but that doesn't mean we like it. No one naturally likes a demerit at work, no one loves to be the one who receives a redo on a project in any of our vocations. We might like the fruit of correction *eventually*, but correction remains at the bottom of our "Things to Do for Fun" list.

What does James have to say about correction in James 4:5-10?

Correction could be defined as: a requirement to submit to the authority in charge, namely our mom or dad, our teachers, our bosses, or our government leaders. Correction also involves listening to those we are influenced by, having and receiving accountability within our relationships. Upon taking in words or actions of correction, our internal spirit vacillates between relief that someone else is in charge and frustration that the one in charge isn't us. We like control, so submission, even in the most submissive of individuals is a task of growth, best done intentionally.

List all the verbs, or action words, James uses in James 4:5-10.

I'm reminded of just how hard it is to get my kids to remember to intentionally wash their hands after using the bathroom, much less the intentional work of submitting to my spouse or my boss. Even when a relationship is with a kind and gentle person, it can be easy to want things the way we want them. I desire to submit to my government leaders as a citizen, but I rarely agree with all of their laws. Any others of you testing the speed limits out there with me?

In reality, when we accept correction from those relationships right in front of us, we are submitting to a Higher Authority. Our big beef with correction, when we get down to it, is that God is in charge and we are not. We like to choose our own path and direct our own ways. However, we simply were not made for that. James uses the best language imaginable for the type of submission that goes with correction in our relationship with God. Look back at James 4:8 and write the first four words of the verse out below –

Now, write it somewhere else in order to remember it and have it in front of you each day. I might even write it on my hand, or my foot, or the top of my knee to remind me that relationship with God means bending said knee and bowing my pretty little head. He is Holy and Mighty and Far Above me. But God operates differently in relationship with Him than He does outside of relationship with Him. When we know Jesus, drawing near means being held, and yes, being corrected.

What does God give us in both the correction and the holding close of draw near, according to James 4:5-6?

Our God is both truth and grace. Correction is hard:

That pinprick of the conscience when we know we've done wrong

Opening our mouth for words of apology when we have spoken too harshly

Walking the hard road because we took our own way the first time around

But take heart! Correction by the Father is always delivered with grace.

He gives more grace.

Forgiveness comes into our lives:

> *If we confess our sins, he is faithful and just to forgive us our sins and to cleanse us from all unrighteousness.*
> *1 John 1:9*

His righteousness comes into our lives. His goodness comes into our lives. His completeness comes into our lives:

> *All Scripture is breathed out by God and profitable for teaching, for reproof, for correction, and for training in righteousness, that the man of God may be complete, equipped for every good work.*
> *2 Timothy 3:16*

Rootedness comes into our lives:

> *Whoever loves discipline loves knowledge,*
> *but he who hates reproof is stupid...*
> *No one is established by wickedness,*
> *but the root of the righteous will never be moved.*
> *Proverbs 12:1,3*

These are all good fruits! These are all God fruits.

He's ready to pick us up when we fall, dust us off, and help us along as we journey the steep and the narrow, the wide and the open, always one day closer and nearer to Him.

He gives more grace.
Let us draw near.

Good Fruit

day four

Different Fruits for Different Folks

What kind of fruit do you most want to shine in your life? When we think of fruit, we most often think of the words of Galatians 5. Read Galatians 5:22-23 and list the fruits you find there.

These are good fruits! These are all God fruits. Which of the Galatians fruits do you see and feel God growing in you in your current season? (Remember: God's Spirit is working, even when don't feel a thing. Look closer.)

I love the Galatians list. It helps me focus in on many of the beautiful gifts God offers me through His Spirit. Is it possible, though, for us to get so caught up in one list of Scripture that we forget God has more fruits?

Look at James 3:17. We've read it before, so it may sound familiar. This time, though, list the fruits mentioned in the verse, just as we did for the Galatians text.

Indeed, the word *fruits* in James 3:17 utilizes the same Greek root word as the one we find for the fruits of the Spirit in Galatians 5 - *karpos*. This word is related to the vine and the branches idea we find in the Gospels. We are part of the same tree. We receive all our nourishment from the vine, who is our Savior. Can you picture yourself grafted into His love and sharing of the same fruit then?

A good definition of biblical fruit is anything done in partnership with Christ. Without Him, it's just not fruit. Consider anything you do in partnership with Christ. In the space below, write down what comes to mind. You can use the lists found in Galatians and James to help you get started, but don't limit yourself to seeking patience – although it's a good fruit, it's not the only fruit. God gives us more grace and more gifts!

It might help to widen our perspective even more. Let's do a good fruits treasure hunt in James. Flip through the entire book of James as a whole. Jot down anything you find people doing in partnership with Christ.

Really what we see when we look at all these lists and books within God's Word is what we call Life Together in action, with Christ and with one another.

Without Christ, joy is incomplete. Joy is also most certainly perceived, understood, and experienced within our Christian walk on this planet, and that includes relationship with other believers. Without Christ, self-control is really just morality, and that eventually breaks down. Self-control also shines best in our relationships with other people. Where better to harness some self-control than with those we love, at work, in church, or in our neighborhoods? In a world that is often anything but gentle, gentleness is just a nice abstract thing, but with Him it ministers to souls.

James 5:13-16 (which we will look at in-depth next week) gives us a vivid picture of life together, turning toward Him together in any and all of life's situations. In James 5:13-16, where and how do you see Jesus working in the people of His Church?

In our suffering, in our prayers, in our leadership, in our praise, we turn one another to Him. Who is part of your tree of fruit from the Lord? Who do you work in partnership with for Christ? Who prays with you? List at least five names of those in your orchard, if you will.

That is good fruit...God fruit.

A Good Future

James 1:16-17
Do not be deceived, my beloved brothers.
Every good gift and every perfect gift is from above,
coming down from the Father of lights,
with whom there is no variation or shadow due to change.

week four

A Good Future

My Slightly Crooked Crown of Life
My Plans and God's Pursuit
What Did God Promise Me?
The Patience of Job or Not So Much

Verse for consideration

Come now, you who say, "Today or tomorrow we will go into such and such a town and spend a year there and trade and make a profit"—yet you do not know what tomorrow will bring. What is your life? For you are a mist that appears for a little time and then vanishes.

James 4:13-14

day one
My Slightly Crooked Crown of Life

My oldest daughter, Macee, and I are avid watchers of the Netflix original show, *The Crown*, which depicts the early reign of Queen Elizabeth the Second in 20th century England. It's a lovely show with deep emotion. It gives lots of different perspectives from many characters of the time period. The queen at the time of the first season is young, and much is thrown at her immediately as she assumes the throne – responsibility, expectations, budgets, and the needs of a nation.

The Crown is just a show, but it brings to mind the *weight* of the crown...any crown. It sounds like a nice idea to be a princess, a queen, a king, or any royalty, but we would be fooling ourselves if we didn't also think it was a job with its own challenges. A crown, even when ceremonial, bears with it the weight of a thousand or more expectations.

James tells us in James 1:12 that we also have a crown. Circle the type of crown followers of Jesus have, according to the Spirit-inspired words of James:

Blessed is the man who remains steadfast under trial, for when he has stood the test he will receive the crown of life, which God has promised to those who love him.

Our crown is different. Our crown isn't a crown of expectation - heavy, overbearing, laden with the jewels of what we need to do or have done. In order to understand the crown of life referenced in James, we need to broaden our scriptural vantage point once again. We'll go out wider to other pieces of Scripture, but first, let's go back and dig around James again. Keeping in mind what we have learned so far in our study, particularly in chapter one, what characteristics of God can be found in the 27 verses of James 1?

Now, look at James 1:12. Consider, in what ways has Jesus been "the man" who has remained steadfast under trial?

We are called to remain steadfast, but we need a foundation in our Savior Jesus remains steadfast under trial. Jesus received the crown of life on Easter morning. Jesus is love itself and loved us first. I think one of the overarching messages of the book of James is this:

God doesn't want to keep it to Himself. God gives good gifts.

This week, we'll settle on the gift He gives us called the future. It's time to zoom out further to consider the whole New Testament picture. Let's look closer at the crown worn on Good Friday. The same Greek word for crown – *stephanon* – used in James 1:12 is also found in each of the following verses. Takes notes next to each verse reference on the context and quality of each of these crowns.

Matthew 27:29

John 19:5

Revelation 14:14

Isn't Jesus so worthy? He took the crown that was full of the weight of death so that we could have life, and really, really LIVE.

Yes, we will have trial and fears, struggle and temptation, but we see life from a crown-bearing perspective. Queen Elizabeth on the show, *The Crown*, had to practice walking with dignity, wearing a gigantic crown on her head, for weeks leading up to her coronation. She wasn't any less queen when the crown shifted to the right because she wasn't an "expert" crown-wearer yet.

The same is true for us in God's kingdom. There are no experts at life and "winners" who receive the crown above others. We don't receive the crown because we lived our challenges better than the guy next to us. We receive it because it is a gift. Crowns, like crosses, occasionally *feel* heavy, but we have a Savior who says,

> *"Come to me, all who labor and are heavy laden, and I will give you rest. Take my yoke upon you, and learn from me, for I am gentle and lowly in heart, and you will find rest for your souls. For my yoke is easy, and my burden is light."*
> *Matthew 11:28-30*

This is a crown of Life, after all. The Greek word for life here - *zoes* - insinuates not just present life but a fuller life that includes the future. Every time we undergo trial, whether a deep and personal struggle or a trial of the everyday variety, we remember our crowns and remember Whose we are. Read 1 Corinthians 9:25-26. How does knowing you have been given the crown of life in Jesus's death and resurrection change the way you run the race?

The crown has been won, the victory secured. Straighten that crown, friend. Look to the future. He's already there. He has this day and every day under His care. And when the world pushes in, we simply reply:

My crown may be slightly crooked, but it's 100% secure.

A Good Future

day two
My Plans and God's Pursuit

Sometimes I think I have good ideas. Well, all the time. I really like my ideas, and I'm full of them. I also am evidently big on honesty. How about you? Are you an idea person?

When we talk about the future, we have to talk about ideas, whether ideas come to us naturally or not. We all need to make some plans in our daily lives – where to go, what to do, what needs attention, and where we'd like to be in five years' time.

Goals are good, but let's hear what James has to say about goals, the future, and our ideas. Hopefully, studying this closer will help us be able to hand our ideas over to God more intentionally as we move through life. He's already got our future in His hands. He already has the control and the very best plans, far better than our own. It's so much easier to walk in those plans He has prepared when we are connected to Him, vine and branches.

In James 4:13-17, what nudge does he give, encouraging us to find a little more peace when it comes to goals and ideas?

James reveals where sin comes in. It's not a sin to have ideas, but it is a sin to boast in those ideas and to put our trust in those ideas. We like our ideas and our plans so much that we leave no room for God's ideas and plans. This creates two problems.

Problem 1: We leave out God.

We think so much of our ideas and plans that no one can see God in them. We move through our lives saying, "I'm going here. I'm doing this. I'm creating this out of my life." We may even look good doing it, because our God doesn't use fire and brimstone to make us aware of our ridiculousness (most of the time). Our lives may be comfortable and they may fit our definition of good, but we sacrifice a closeness with God that we get when we lean into Him and into His Word and listen for His ideas and plans. When we are only tuned into on our own plans and ideas, we can only see us. We are less likely to pray, to seek His Word and insight. Life may be a-ok, but we've given our days away and missed the very best part – conversation and active relationship with Jesus Christ. Additionally, no one else can see Him in a life lived only for ourselves and our plans.

Problem 2: We take the long route.

We end up walking the long way around, up the mountain, through the fire, and sometimes into the pit, to get to the path God would have showed us to begin with. Most of us have known this pain at one time or another. Have you ever walked the hard road to a destination God was trying to lead you to gently? God pursues us on any road. He knows His sheep. He loves His sheep. When have you seen God's faithful pursuit in your life?

God will chase us down to help us find the path He has chosen for us. Where Psalm 23:6 uses the term *follow* in many translations, someone pointed out to me recently that it also means *pursue*. Isn't it good to know we have a God who won't give up on us, even when we're looking every which way but up? We can, of course, take this too far. We don't believe God will be chasing us down to make sure we take a left turn to go to the grocery store. He might intervene very uniquely in each of our lives, but His primary concern for plans and ideas is that we know Jesus Christ as our Lord and Savior.

James firmly turns us to prayer, again and again. What plans do you have today? What ideas would you really like to see come to fruition? Turn to Him in conversation and prayer. Open His Word and see what He says. Present your requests, your ideas, and your plans to Him, knowing that He is a God who pursues, who knows best, who gives generously from a wise and steadfast heart.

A Good Future

day three
What did God Promise Me?

I'm old enough, with enough grey hair, to look out at our culture and see our expectations of God are out of control. We don't want a God who judges our thoughts and actions harshly, but we also don't want a God who lets the sins of other people slide. We want God to intervene, but we also want Him to leave us alone when it comes to our own sin. We want Him to fix things in our lives, but we want to be in charge of our own lives. How do you see these ideas play out in the culture around you and in your own life?

Very often, we are so much like little children when it comes to God. We want what we want, how we want it, and when we want it. James, again, wants us to have a congruent picture of God, as well as a congruent walk of faith. He's very concerned with who God is really, according to Scripture, not our picture of Him.

Chapter 5 of the book of James addresses the subject of promises. Promises are those things we hold God to, what we want from Him, and what we expect from Him. What promise of God is found in James 5:7-8?

What other promises does God make to us in Scripture? Look up the following passages and rest in His sure and certain promises.

Luke 12:6-7

Romans 8:38-39

2 Peter 3:9

Jeremiah 29:11

James 5:7-8 is found in the middle of a chapter and section of Scripture about wealth, security, patience, and trust. Read James 5:1-10 and consider the following questions:

What do richness or wealth have to do with patience or impatience?

What grumbling may come against our brother because of wealth of any kind?

What did the prophets fight for in the name of the Lord and what does this have to do with patience? What does it have to do with wealth?

I can't say it enough – in this world we like stuff. We value stuff. Because of that, even if we're not really "stuff" people, we want stuff from God and we inadvertently hold Him to promises He never made.

We look at our neighbors house and think - "Well, God, they have nicer things. Why, God? What's wrong with me, God? I'm faithful."

We look at our neighbor's family and think - "Well, God, their children are well-behaved. Why, God? What's wrong with me, God? I follow you."

We look at our neighbors' lives and think, "They have it so much easier. Where's their burden, Lord? Where's their struggle? Why are You giving me less, Lord?"

Our internal dialogue can certainly help us understand our need for Jesus at times. Here's the Truth:

God promised Jesus.

That's it. End of sentence. All His promises, and there are many, could be wrapped up into that one single promise. God promised Jesus. No matter what else we want from Him, this is the promise that everything stands on. If it isn't about Jesus, there's an incredibly good chance God didn't promise it.

If we look deep down at what we want from God and don't come up with Jesus in there, or something related to Jesus, it was never really promised to begin with.

James 5:8 tells us simply and eloquently -

Establish your hearts, for the coming of the Lord is at hand.

Everything, the wealth of our hands, the abundance of our fields and tables, and any lack of what we might think of as good in our lives – any one thing, any season, any place, any deficiency in our world, is a flashing red light pointing us to Christ.

Jesus is the promise.

In the struggle, I see Jesus tend to me. The Lord is at hand.

In the abundance, I see Jesus' overflowing love. The Lord is at hand.

In the early rains, I see Jesus' plans spring up. The Lord is at hand.

In the late rains, I see Jesus' perseverance and pursuit of me. The Lord is at hand.

What promises are you asking of God today? Hold them out before Him. Ask yourself and ask God in prayer,

Is this about Jesus?

That's a promise you can hold God to.

Lord, give us your Spirit, give us forgiveness, and give us Jesus. Amen.

A Good Future

day four

The Patience of Job or Not So Much

Sometimes I wonder if the people who reference the patience of Job (pronounced J-oh-b) have ever really read the book of Job in the Bible. Job is a human, and in being such, he only has so much patience. The book of Job is quite a comfort for someone afflicted with just about anything, because Job was afflicted with just about everything. Let's hear a little from our friend, Job, and then we'll get to James. Read the following passages from Job and sum up his struggles in your own words.

Job 3:11-13

Job 14:1-3

Job 23:2-4

This is me taking Job slightly out of context and that's not fair. Job vacillates back and forth between praise and trust, lament and insecurity, just like we often do in our own lives. Our walks also include frustration, anger, understanding, angst, hope, questions, and joy. Job is a child of God, imperfect, but redeemed, just as we are.

Let's look at where James and Job meet in James 5:8-11. The first part of this passage overlaps with where we left off in the last lesson. What word or words does James use to describe Job in the passage?

Job is not in the Bible because he was patient. He's in the Bible because he was steadfast.

The Bible never said that Job wasn't angry, didn't have to confront ugly emotions, nor does it tell us he had great answers for himself or his friends. He simply gave God an open place to work, and that's what we can do as well.

"You have heard of the steadfastness of Job..."

We live an imperfect life with lots of bitter and lots of sweet. Steadfastness is holding fast, clinging to that which we know through both. Job's story also gives us insight in how to cling when life is hard, as well as when it's wonderful. Look up the following passages from Job and find four gifts God gives us to remain steadfast, even when we aren't necessarily patient.

Gift 1: The Lord is steadfast.

What steadfastness is displayed in Job 10:11-13?

Gift 2: We have the Steadfast Word.

What adjectives describe God and His Word in Job 23:10-12?

Gift 3: Eternity is real and steadfast.

What promises can be found in Job 19:25-27?

Gift 4: We are given the steadfast Holy Spirit.

How does the Spirit bring steadfastness into our lives according to Job 27:2-4?

Like Job, I say and will probably continue to say ridiculous things in my days, particularly on the hard ones, the bitter ones, and the sad ones, but the Holy Spirit gives me breath and life, His Word keeps me grounded, and His Son keeps me fixed on all those blessed tomorrows of Eternity with Him, rather than the struggle of the moment.

In James 5:11, Job is mentioned once, but James draws our attention to the Lord by repeating His name twice.

The Lord has a purpose for us.

The Lord is compassionate toward us.

The Lord is merciful to us.

In the bitter and in the sweet of life, the Lord does not fail. He is steadfast today, yesterday, and tomorrow.

Good Relationships

James 1:16-17
Do not be deceived, my beloved brothers.
Every good gift and every perfect gift is from above,
coming down from the Father of lights,
with whom there is no variation or shadow due to change.

week five

Good Relationships

The Good Gift of We
What Does Friendship with God Look Like?
Brothers, Sisters, Chief of Sinners, Jedi
The Invitation to Draw Near

Verse for consideration

You also, be patient. Establish your hearts, for the coming of the Lord is at hand.

James 5:8

Good Relationships

day one

The Good Gift of We

Have you been enjoying the book of James? James's words, guided by the Spirit of Truth and Grace, contain some tough Law and some meaty Gospel. The book of James gives us a chance to wrestle with the two.

Over the next five days of study, we'll focus on relationship – one of my very favorite topics. We were made for relationship and I think you'll see that this is something James knew and understood well. More than that, James also clearly valued relationship. He saw the local church as a community living life together, hearing and doing the Word together, and reaching out to pray with and for one another – together. James encourages those in God's church to share words which cared for the soul, as well as the mind, and to sharpen one another through all kinds of storms by compassionately and gently pointing each other to God and His Word rather than letting one another walk this road of life alone.

Look at the theme verse of our entire study again, this time to connect the words and wisdom in James with the value of relationships. Read James 1:16-18 and write down any words that connect James in relationship with the readers of the time and today, or God with His people.

James centers his own relationship, as well as the relationship he has with those he is writing to, on our God who connects us, our good and holy Father. Our relationship as brothers isn't just as people living next to one another, attending church next to one another, even sitting in struggle next to one another. Our relationship is firmly planted in the simple but full fact that we are children of the same Father. And we are beloved, not only by James's proclamation, but even this adjective is an indicator of something about our good God. Humankind was made and created by a Creator Father who loves His creation. But even more sure and certain, is God's love for His adopted sons and daughters – never shifting or changing in Christ Jesus. In the church, we are a family held together by the love of our Savior. What do the following verses tell us about the Father's love for us, as well as His desire to have relationship with us?

Romans 8:15

Galatians 4:7-9

1 John 3:1-2

1 John 4:19

We are all brothers once through creation, but as believers we are brothers twice through our adoption as sons in Christ Jesus. James took "beloved brothers" seriously. His genuineness shines when you look throughout the book at the sheer quantity of times he refers to his listener as *brother*. Here's a fun challenge – flip through the book of James and note every time he uses the term brother, either by journaling each verse on white space offered at the end of today's study, or by underlining or highlighting them in your Bible.

You might have noted that there is at least one reference to *brothers* in every chapter of James. He knows that to be heard by his reader, the relationship matters. He isn't manipulative. He is aware. He is speaking to people he knows as part of the same Body. By calling them brothers, he reminds them of the covenant relationship they were gifted by our great God. I think *brothers* just flowed out of James's pen as an honest statement of unity. Notice he often couples the term with the endearment *beloved.* Beloved speaks of life and love, of holding one another's hand in the storm, of "in it together" rather than shame and pointing fingers.

In the Apostle Paul's writings throughout the Epistles, you will find similar language. Slide over to any Bible app and use the search engine to input the term *brothers*. How many times do you see it in the books of Paul - Romans, Corinthians, Thessalonians, Philippians, etc. Do you notice how many times the word *brothers* is used in the whole of Scripture? That's a lot of brotherly affection. It's important to note that James isn't excluding anyone within the Body of Christ either. James uses *brothers* as a general term encompassing women as well. It is a cultural way of speaking, appropriate for the time in which the book was written.

We are in this together, brothers and sisters. James knew it, Paul knew it. We know it. How are we living it? What does life lived together look like? Partly, it just is. We can't change our relationship. We are affected by one another, by our words, our actions, our choices, because it's how God made us. But I think part of it is what Jesus refers to as *the abundant life* in John 10:10. What He came to give us is salvation, but remember He gives more grace. He also gives us the knowledge of just how beautiful life as brothers can be. To close our study today, let's meditate on Psalm 133. It's short and sweet but compliments our study of this topic well. Read the Psalm and consider – who do you dwell with in life together? Who is in your circle of brothers and sisters in creation and in Christ? Write their names beside the Psalm and then lift them up in prayer.

> *Behold, how good and pleasant it is*
> *when brothers dwell in unity!*
> *It is like the precious oil on the head,*
> *running down on the beard,*
> *on the beard of Aaron,*
> *running down on the collar of his robes!*
> *It is like the dew of Hermon,*
> *which falls on the mountains of Zion!*
> *For there the Lord has commanded the blessing,*
> *life forevermore.*
>
> *Psalm 133*

Unity isn't perfection of communication, never having a different of opinion or wrestling with difficult topics. It is love. It is noticing one another. It is life lived alongside and truly in one another's lives, rather than as ships passing in the night.

Lord, use us, in the power of your Spirit, to be true brothers and sisters to those around us. Give us strength in the drama and the mess to invite others in and to seek and give care and affection. You, Lord, are our Brother. We hold fast to that Word of truth in all we say and do. In Jesus' name. Amen.

Good Relationships

day two
What Does Friendship with God Look Like?

Maslow's hierarchy of needs has long been the standard for understanding human needs. Maslow taught that people need the basics of life – water, food, shelter, safety – before they can begin to trouble themselves with the higher needs of love, belonging, esteem, and self-actualization or personal fulfillment. While there is some truth in this, I have been encouraged to see some amount of research across recent years acknowledging for the world out there what we know as Christians - connection isn't secondary, especially connecting with our Savior.

We may not be able to survive without food, but to some extent what kind of survival is that without connection, without someone to share it with. When we worked with a feeding program as part of the wholistic mission of Ministry in Mission in Haiti, the children didn't just come for the food and juice, they came to be loved on, to sing songs together, and to see what Hope looks like from people who shared Jesus with them. I'm positive they would have shown up without the food offered. The food was a much needed provision for the children, as well as the adults caring for them…but so was the connection. We were created by a Good Father for connection with Him above all else.

It can be easy to think of friendship and connection mostly within the horizontal realm, in our family and friendships with one another, because they are right in front of our faces. But what we believe about God, our vertical friendship with God, affects what we believe, think, and how we act in our friendships with one another. He created friendship. He created every good thing we might encounter on this earth to be shared in relationship *with* Him, never apart from Him. This means that if we want quality friendships with one another, we need to understand our friendship with God first.

James sheds a little light on what friendship with God means and looks like for us. Let's open to James 2. Take a minute to read the entire chapter for context. Then write out James 2:1 in the space below.

Partiality is something our sinful natures are prone to as humans. Impartiality is found in the person and work of Jesus Christ. True friendship, that given to us by God in Jesus, offers impartiality, safety and care, and extends the hand of fellowship enough to know someone deeper, beyond a meet and greet. On earth, our friendships often begin with,

"You too?!"

But Christ's brand of friendship teaches us they can also begin with,

"Tell me more."
"You are worthy of time and energy."
"How can I help?"

John 15:12-15 are the red-letter words of Jesus on love and friendship. What do we learn about this topic from Jesus in this passage?

James helps us see our friendship with God on a deeply personal level, by pointing us to Abraham in James 2:19-23. Humor me: What title does James remind us God used with Abraham?

In Genesis 18, Abraham was blessed to meet with God. Through Christ's sacrifice on the cross, and the benefit of His Word available to us daily, we also can meet with Him at any moment, in any day. When we read James 2:19-23, we could easily only hear James's recurring phrase "Faith without works, faith without works, faith without works..." in our head, but in this instance, *works* can easily be summed up in this: relationship. That relationship we read about in John 15, flowing from God the Father, through Christ, to us, and out to one another is the foundation of how we understand the intimacy we call friendship.

Read Genesis 18:1-15 and see what kind of relationship God offered to Abraham so many years ago, which He offers to us today.

First, the Lord visits us.

Read Genesis 18: 1-5. What actions or words are shared on the visit that stand out to you?

Just as God did not find it offensive to come to Abraham's tent, partake of Abraham's food, and rest in Abraham's company, he similarly exists with us. We need only open His Word, talk about Him in our day, and share what He's doing and done in our lives through Jesus to be visited by the Most High God. He wants to visit with us. He doesn't impose a time limit on our time together. He visits us in our worship and invites us to His table to share His meal.

Second, God converses with us.

Read Genesis 18:9-15. What was the conversation between Abraham, Sarah, and the visitors concerning?

I LOVE this exchange in Scripture. This passage could be much shorter and to the point, but instead God gives us many details, even the humorous details. The interaction between Abraham and Sarah reminds me I don't have to have it all together to meet with God. It also reminds me He'll straighten me out in His Truth and His Love when I've got my head in the sand. My God, my Friend, welcomes me to the conversation for the delight of relationship, and in Him I find restoration for my soul.

Last, we are given great and precious promises in our Savior.

What did Abraham and Sarah receive? The seed which is Christ Jesus. This seed was promised to two people that God dared call friends – who had their issues, who were themselves sinners – but also actively received grace from the God that gives more grace, just like us. This seed came to fruition in Bethlehem to save us all, but don't miss the grace of God choosing to simply have a conversation with two very regular believers near those oak trees so long ago.

Come, Lord Jesus. Eat our food. Be our Guest. Rest in our homes with us. Recline at our tables in Your open Word. Make full our hearts and lives in conversation and friendships centered on you.

I am a friend of God.

You are a friend of God.

Good Relationships

day three

Brothers, Sisters, Chief of Sinners, Jedi

I'll let you in on a little secret: I love talking about Star Wars. If you follow any of my writing or any of my videos, my podcast, even my social media, it won't take you long to figure out how much I love talking about Star Wars.

I own shirts, notebooks, and a waffle maker that express my vibrant love for all things dark side and light side. I listen to various Star Wars podcasts and daydream about being a guest interviewee. People that visit our toy room frequently comment, "Wow, your kids like Star Wars." It's true. My husband also loves to talk about Star Wars, so we easily passed on the obsession to our offspring. But don't worry, we try to pass on more Jesus than Star Wars, so they'll be ok.

What does Star Wars have to do with Bible study? How can this movie franchise find a space in our little study of James? Because, this side of heaven, the good gift of relationships has a truth we cannot ignore:

Life together has a dark side.

Very often, the center of that dark side is personal judgement.

Personal judgement is different from the righteous judgement of God. God, as perfect Creator, perfect Redeemer, and perfect Counselor has every right to judge.

The world, however, is imperfect. You are imperfect and I am imperfect. But people love to share their opinions and suggestions just as much as I love to talk about Star Wars, and we like to throw an edge on our opinions by adding judgment that doesn't belong to us, but really is the place of the Lord and His Word. If you are having a hard time identifying what I'm talking about, just go check out any social media thread. If we cannot share our judgements personally, we'll throw them on the internet.

While they didn't have social media, James had many of the same relationship concerns for the people in the early church that we have today. What does James say about judging in James 4:10-12?

Note: sharing truth in love is not the dark side.

James loved his brothers. That much is evident from our study yesterday. Brotherly love and affection, however, does not mean the absence of truth. James doesn't trade in hard truths for untruth. He says it like it is. It's one of the hardest parts about reading and studying James. But he couches every statement, every Law, and every piece of Gospel in the language of *we*, recognizing everyone's need for forgiveness and salvation, including his own.

Judgement, however, is when we make our own rules, when we share our own opinions on life choices rather than God's, when we share God's Word even, but absent from love, or when we assume a deep relationship we haven't put the effort into creating and sustaining in order to share truth and love together. Sharing truth involves follow through and follow up. Judgment is alive and well when we fail to recognize our own need for forgiveness. This is the humility James is speaking of in James 4:10.

Brothers is just what we are in this Body of Christ, but James teaches us that we are brothers in more ways than one.

We are brothers in sin.

Saying it like that, out loud, sounds terrible. But it is our earthly reality. We may not like hearing it, but hearing that truth together is also how we get to the grace together. We are imperfect. Our brother is imperfect. Our families are imperfect. Praise God we have a perfect Savior. Only by identifying *together* our state of imperfection can we begin to talk to one another about the things that matter most- with love, and kindness, affection and humility.

We are brothers in need of a Savior.

It's not that our sins are the same, but our hearts are in the same condition. We NEED Jesus. We NEED Him in a way that brings us to a place where we not only desperately need His salvation, but we also desperately need the support of one another.

How does hearing Paul's personal testimony of his own sinfulness and need for salvation in 1 Timothy 1:13-16 offer encouragement for your day today, in your own sinfulness and need for salvation?

Life together helps us to see our own need, rather than our own superiority. Chief of sinners though we be, we are forgiven, redeemed, and set free. He walked out of the tomb so that we could help one another dance, walk, and hobble down the road, chains broken, lives restored.

Sinners together. Forgiven together. We have a Father of Light.

day four
The Invitation to Draw Near

God is jealous for us. While this is verbalized throughout the Old Testament, I think because we live after the incarnation of Jesus, and the resurrection of Jesus, we often imagine a placid God, a God who is only peace and never jealousy. Let's not rob Him of His character though. God has a right to be jealous. He reigns inside our hearts with His Spirit. As baptized followers, He has set us apart for His work. He has called us by our name. We are His.

James reminds us of the jealousy still found in our New Testament God. He is jealously passionate for our souls. He will not allow the devil to have any power in our lives lightly, or without purpose.

Read James 4:5-8. Classify the actions taken in this passage under who they apply to – God or us.

God   Us

Jesus' grace stands between us and the righteous jealousy of God. With that in mind, all the promises found in James 4:5-8 could be summed up in a single statement, found in verse 8.

Draw Near...

I do not think you could find a more relationship-oriented action if you tried. God draws near to us in His incarnation. Jesus walked our soil. He drew near by taking our sins on His shoulders to bear the load and redeem us. Then God drew near by sending His Spirit into our hearts and our lives, recorded in the book of Acts. Individually, He draws so near that He chose you as His dwelling place. What Scripture quotation is found in James 4:5?

How do we talk about drawing any nearer to our God? James gives us a hearty suggestion in James 5:13-20. What instances and what actions give us a clear opportunity to draw us closer to God, according to James 5:13-20?

One of the most common requests I hear from women and men looking for a way to grow their faith, "Do you know of any resources that will help me grow in my prayer life?"

Absolutely! This is an area I think we'd all like to grow in. Don't feel less than or ostracized if you feel you lack in prayer. It isn't God's way to point His finger at you and shame you. Instead, listen as he whispers in your ear...

Draw Near...

Just do it. Make time for it. Hear the Gospel call of

Draw Near...

Add prayer in snippets into your life and in great gulfs of time in your day. Look back at James words in James 5:13-20. Prayer reflected in the immediate needs of the day as well as prayers of drawn across a season or a lifetime.

There's no one right way. There isn't. Jesus gives us the Lord's Prayer and we would be wise to utilize it. Beyond that I can only share a few ways I have seen make a difference in my personal prayer life and those of others. I've learned from wiser people, who have much more to teach than I, we move towards growing up in faith and drawing near together, each of us growing in our place.

Whisper breath prayer
Pray in the moment when it comes to the surface for you. Snatch that prayer up. Share it with the Lord immediately. Don't let it pass by unnoticed. The Spirit intercedes for us in groans that words cannot express. We are also given grace upon grace to draw near by sharing our thoughts and words intentionally with God.

Pray with others, rather than just for others
One day we went to Guatemala, and I learned to pray. I could go into detail, but there's no time here. It was uncomfortable. It was heart-wrenching. It was exhausting. It was awesome. Next time you are in a conversation with someone and they share something, offer to pray for them, yes. But offer to pray with them. Right there. It's a stretch. You need the Spirit for this, and oh, will He work!

Utilize a prayer journal

Sybil MacBeth on her website, Praying in Color, describes why utilizing visual prayer can help us to draw near and grow in our faith. Our minds are a wonderful thing, but the devil would like to use every barrier to distract us from tending to our relationship with God. Our brains were made to fully engage when we connect one sense to another, connecting our thoughts to audio or visual or tactical experiences brings us into fuller attention during our time with God.

Pray out loud for a set period of time

Set a timer and just start praying. Get a little lost in your prayer so that you're surprised when the timer goes off. Make a gratitude list. Jot down three prayers a day for a week at least. Pick up a prayer tool at visualfaithmin.org.

However you do it, hear the invitation of *draw near* and pull a seat up to the table with God.

You are invited in – to His Word, to His love, in His Spirit, and by His grace.

Draw Near.

Good Word(s)

James 1:16-17
Do not be deceived, my beloved brothers.
Every good gift and every perfect gift is from above,
coming down from the Father of lights,
with whom there is no variation or shadow due to change.

week six

Good Word(s)

The Implanted Word
Embracing Slow
Making Waves
Set the World Ablaze

Verse for consideration

Is anyone among you suffering? Let him pray. Is anyone cheerful? Let him sing praise. Is anyone among you sick? Let him call for the elders of the church, and let them pray over him, anointing him with oil in the name of the Lord.

James 5:13-14

The Implanted Word

I love a good presentation, especially one with a wealth of information, given in fifteen minutes or so. I love finding nuggets of wisdom whether it be in person, on an audio download, while browsing video media sites online – you name it. If it requires a notebook and pencil, I'm in. My favorite things to learn about are the Bible, neurobiology and therapeutic methods, emotions, and nature. How about you? What are your favorite things to learn about?

Recently, I listened to a presentation in my podcast line-up about finding architectural and technological design answers by investigating biology in nature. The presenter identified intricate designs within the natural world, such as beehives or bird's nests, and encouraged listeners to replicate the patterns in their building and program designs.

Presentations on science usually make me simultaneously very excited and very sad. Looking at the way God designed creation to exist and to thrive is a beautiful thing. So often, though, the presenters are so busy seeing the beauty of the created thing, that they almost always miss the Designer Himself.

The stars are placed in the sky...by our Good Father's hands.

The oceans waves acquiesce to the seashore...by our Good Father's command.

The flowers unfold their color...by our Good Father's direction.

Today, we are not going to miss the Designer. We'll praise His name, as well as His design.

Just as God plants trees and flowers, He plants His Word. Just as bushes sprout from seed at their inception, the Word isn't merely handed to us or even read to us, it's planted in us by the true Creator and Designer, Author and Master Gardener of our lives. He designed His Word letter by letter, writer by writer, book by book, and then planted it in us to teach us about who Jesus is and what He's done for us. It is designed to build us up and to spur us on as the people of God.

What instructions do you find in James 1:19-21? How are they related to the Word of God?

In this passage, James uses the Word to help us change the way we use words with one another. During this last week of study, I want to move through the book of James again to set our feet firmly on the Good Gift of words and The Word, planted in us for a purpose.

James 1:21 tells us that God implants His word in our hearts and our minds. The Greek phrase for *implanted word* in the passage above is *emphyton logon*. If you have a notebook or Bible out, write that Greek phrase next to the text "implanted word." Other translation possibilities for *implanted* include: rooted, ingrown, natural, engrafted, or congenital. Implanted is a very good translation and reflects on the work God is doing in us. You can look around in your Bible and find other Bible passages referring to God rooting, God growing, and God engrafting. They are all inner-related. God's work is a process, not an instant product. Reflecting on two words in particular gives us a better understanding of the implanting James refers to.

God's Word is *rooted* in us.

God digs deep into our hearts and lives and places His Word firmly in us. To bring it to a more personal level consider these questions:

How long have you been attending church - since childhood, just recently?

Do you have memories of a grandma or a faithful someone who shared the Word with you?

Now take one of those memories, a vivid one that you have of someone sharing the Word with you. Describe it using all five of your senses.

God works the Word into our life in so many ways – and very often we may not even consciously see it. We hear the Word when we show up to church week after week, even when our ears aren't attentive. Have you ever saved up notes or cards from someone that encouraged you with His Word? Those are roots. Do you have a verse of Scripture that rises up from somewhere within you, from a voice you can't identify (cough-cough...the Holy Spirit)? Those are roots.

One of my favorite people on the planet, Miss Ardyth, faithfully taught my kids songs during the Midweek program at our church for several years. What stuck out to me about Miss Ardyth's song selection was that they were always straight from Scripture. My kids were unknowingly memorizing Scripture and singing them all over the house without even thinking about it. Miss Ardyth believed Psalm 119 and taught me to trust in the power of God's Word tucked deep inside of me.

Look at Psalm 119 for yourself. It's a big one, the longest Psalm in the Psalmody. What promises do you hear in skimming through the verses?

Psalm 119:11 speaks exactly to God's implanting the Word in each of us. Circle the differences in each translation below:

> I have stored up your word in my heart,
>   that I might not sin against you. (ESV)

> I have hidden your word in my heart
>   that I might not sin against you. (NIV)

> I treasure your word in my heart,
>   so that I may not sin against you. (NRSV)

When we hear the Word, when we read the Word, even when we speak the Word, God is storing it, God is hiding it in us, God is building a treasure store in our hearts and minds. This is God planting the Word and the Word taking root.

God's Word *blooms* out of us.

God's Word also just blooms up and comes out. That's the way it's designed. When it's tucked deep inside, rooted with feet and legs, it jumps out when we least expect it. It grabs ahold of us in our need, and it clings tightly to our neighbor whether they understand what exactly the Word is saying to them or not. It grows up and out and brings answers where there were none. It gives comfort where only anxiety had been.

When have you seen the Word bloom? Share a specific instance if you can think of one. Use all the senses again if you can.

Here's a promise you can hold onto today: God's Word never returns void. The Word is rooted and blooming even as you read this. Sit back and watch Him grow.

Good Word(s)

day two
Embracing Slow

To some degree, we all value fast:

Fast internet.

Fast service.

Fast travel.

Fast responses.

What are some of the things you like to receive quickly?

We have people to see and places to go, work to be done. Productivity and innovation travel at lightspeed. Sometimes … it's just exhausting.

I am beginning to understand the value of *slow*. I have also begun to see more articles and news media about the health benefits of slowing down, taking a moment, and embracing rest for the benefit of our minds and bodies. Maybe we're all starting to catch on to the value of rest, even if we often have a hard time practicing it.

Slowing down our words, however – that's another story. When was the last time you read anything on the internet about slowing down what we have to say?

Some of us, myself included, have a lot to say and it all just comes gushing out. Social media can easily encourage this choo-choo train approach to communication with instant likes coupled with the lack of face-to-face feedback.

Say what you think!

Get it off your chest!

You'll feel so much better!

I have had the devil whispering these very things in my ear. He placates our consciences to shove thoughts about how to say something well, how to speak considerately, way down deep. The enemy's false promises are keeping us from looking for the best perspective, speaking in love, and keeping the listener in mind. Then, once the deed is done and the words are out, the guilt and shame begin. The devil sure does pour shame on thick, too.

James gives us a simple and direct suggestion, that we would be wise to heed:

We can be bold, to stand up for what matters, but it doesn't hurt to slow down.

Read James 1:19-20 and write James's simple commands in order of their appearance within the verses:

Conversations start with listening and sharing. Then the discussion gets going and the words come faster. We start to hear less and then we start to speak more. Slow is such a simple concept, we could miss it if we didn't sit on the passage for a moment. God shows us the value He places on *slow* by the way He compiled Scripture first through the Prophets and then the Apostles over the course of many, many years. The words of the Bible were offered slowly, over the sands of time, not hastily through a single individual. God understands time differently from us, as He has no need of it. However, from our standpoint as linear beings, God *took His time* with the Word. James's words are part of the Holy Book, brought forth over time, breathed out by the Trinity.

Let's look through a few more passages in James, keeping them in the context of *slow*. What other wisdom on this does James have to offer around the concept of slowing down our words?

James 2:16

James 3:2-5,8-9

James 4:11a

James 5:12-13

Slow may look a little different from the way the world around us communicates, but isn't that just God's way? May your ways be slow and your words be filled with His praise today.

Good Word(s)

day three
Making Waves

I love the ocean's roll.

I love sitting on the beach, with my feet dug into the sand, the waves reaching up to lap my toes. Waves are calming and predictable – coursing in and out, in and out.

Waves aren't just billowy and pretty though. They are powerful and majestic. They are driven by an unseen force, governed by gravity and the laws of physics. However, we've all seen instances where even the laws of physics can't contain the ocean's power. They are ruled by Someone greater. Someone whom even the wind and waves obey.

Let's explore what waves have to do with James and what they have to do with our words.

Open to James 3:1-5. Who is given instructions in this passage?

James never actually talks about waves, does he? But he does talk about rudders. The moon makes waves, gravity and all kinds of scientific processes make waves, but so do the rudders. When boats pass through the water, they churn up all kinds of stuff. Now, it's easy when instructions are given to a specific group to think - "Eh, I don't teach, so I'm just going to skip over that part." But let's be honest - we all have someone to "teach", someone to influence, someone with whom we share wisdom, life experiences, and God's Word. We are foolish if we believe that we impact no one as we move through life. I guarantee you that your impact, my friend, is bigger than you think! We each have reach and possibility and many relationships in our lives. Our tongue guides much of this. How do we even begin to steer our tongues in the right direction? How do we find a direction that creates safety and spreads the message of Hope, instead of messages of fear and of judgment?

The question is not, are we making waves with our lives and words? Rather, it's –

What kind of waves are we making?

Are we drowning others? Are we saying what we want, when we want? Are we letting the emotions of the moment and satisfaction in our "rightness" steal hope from someone else's soul? Are we ruled by our tongue, or do we let the Spirit guide our words, even when we are hurt, angry, tired, or hungry? Are we slowly eroding the beach? Are our words not often harsh, but edgy – sarcastic enough, selfish enough – to tear down rather than build up, over time? Do we avoid, rather than seek, opportunities to speak up for others?

Or are we bringing God's good change to a dark world? Do we give care, affection, or grace, through our words? Do we let the Spirit speak to whomever He brings into our life? Do our words roll up and reach out to someone's shore, lapping their feet with the warmth and love of Christ?

We won't be perfect. Our words won't be perfect. But we are learning to trust the refining to Him along the journey.

Lord, show us where You are leading us and where our ship is plunging ahead without Your mercy and grace. Thank You for Your wisdom and truth, as well as Your forgiveness, always there for us. Fill us with Your Spirit, for the adventure of each day. In Christ, we give all our words to You. Use them for Your glory alone. In Jesus' name, Amen.

day four

Set the World Ablaze

Yesterday, we talked about making waves.

Today we're going to talk about setting a blaze.
In James 3:5-8, our author gets fiery. What is the impact of our words in connection to fire, according to James?

Notice the connecting piece between our segment yesterday, the waves, and what we are studying today, fire. Write out James 3:5 in the space below.

How does the tongue find trouble on its own sometimes, without our help?

James points out the fact that our tongues can set the world ablaze, but they need to be bridled and steered. The Greek word for *unrighteousness* in the ESV translation of James 3:6 is *adikias*, from the root word *adikia*, which can also refer to injustice and hurt. That hits the nail on the head. Fires can be glorious – but also destructive.

How is our tongue downright hurtful sometimes?

Ephesians 4:14-16 speaks similarly about waves and wind and selfish words. How do we grow up and out of them, according to this passage?

We are not tossed like people with no guidance system. We have Jesus living in us. We are driven by the Holy Spirit and by God's Word. In Christ, we are not left to idle in a sea of doubt and chaos. We have Hope.

God's Word says that two things ignite - truth and love. So, we can ask ourselves two questions before we open our mouth...

Am I speaking truth? Am I speaking love?

It sounds too simple. But God knows that it's just so easy for us to speak one without the other. One won't work...ever. We need both questions:

Am I speaking truth?

Am I speaking love with no truth?

Brothers and sisters, if we are aiming for setting the world on fire for Christ, we are intended to speak both as one.
I fail miserably at this: Children, pick up your toys! Husband, plan a date night! Friend, pick up the phone and text me! So

many necessary commands that might speak truth, but unfortunately I forget to include the love. It's easy when we are in a conversation with a friend about their struggle with a specific sin to speak only love and care - "It's ok! It's no big deal!" – without the truth that they so desperately need in order to see Christ's forgiveness and love. It's also easy to speak only judgment – "You should have...Why didn't you..." – with little or no compassion.

Where do you have the hardest time with sharing truth with love and love with truth?

Reread James 3:8. What comfort do you find there?

Don't blink or you'll miss it. You are not the first, nor will you be the last, to struggle with tongue-taming. It's a daily work of sanctification. Christ's mercy was given to us on the cross. It works in us every day, to set fires that point to His Life, rather than death and destruction. We will daily struggle with this, but it's a good work, a good walk with our Savior who knows boundless grace.

Work that good Grace in us today, Lord. Truth in love and love in truth – we leave it at Your feet every day. Set some fires around us in Your name, for Your glory. Amen.

A STUDY OF JAMES

Heidi Goehmann

A NOTE OF THANKS

Thank you for studying with me! If you have any thoughts, questions, or would like permission to copy a portion of this book, please contact the author, Heidi Goehmann, LCSW, LIMHP, deaconess on the About page at heidigoehmann.com. I would love to hear from you! You can also follow me on my Facebook page – Heidi Goehmann Writes, on Instagram by following @heidigoehmann, and follow me on snapchat by following @heidiadventures. Find complimentary videos to accompany this study on the Heidi Goehmann Writes YouTube channel. You can always find me, as well as articles and resources for mental health, genuine relationships, and hope in Jesus at heidigoehmann.com

Dave, Macee, Jonah, Jyeva, and Ezekiel – I can't thank you enough for your encouragement and the grace you give me.

Thank you to Sarah for her time and energy in not only editing this text, but always working through the studies with me from the time they are just tiny ideas inside my head until they are a book you can hold.

Thank you to Melissa for graphics that make the text inviting and easy to follow, and working, reworking, and working again until we find just the right graphic touch.

Thank you to my readers who participated in the online version of this study. Your comments, suggestions, and input greatly impacted the final outcome of this study and gave it energy and life.

Made in the USA
Monee, IL
20 May 2021